Praise for *Wake Up*

When people discover you're a writer, probably the first thing they ask you is, "Where do you get your ideas?" and you reply, "They're everywhere!" But what if you're a writer, and suddenly your mind goes blank. What do you do then? Simple! You pick up Jan Christiansen's Wake Up Your Muse. With 1001 story starters such as "The elevator jerked to a stop, the lights flickered, and five strangers were about to spend a very long night together" and "Her hands shook as she read her own birth certificate," you will never run out of ideas again.

> *- Donna Clark Goodrich, author of A Step in the Write Direction—the Complete How-to Book for Christian Writers. www.thewritersfriend.net*

Ah, the story starter! As both an author and creative writing teacher, I've learned to depend on these fun prompts to stir up creativity. Jan Christiansen's book is loaded with great story starters, sure to get the creative ball rolling. Perfect for writers, teachers and students, alike.

> *- Janice Hanna Thompson, author of "Creative Writing for the Christian Student"*

This book is something I can use to jump start a story, find a creative twist on a scene, or discover a different facet of my writing voice. What a great resource for any writer who's feeling creatively dry or like they're in a story rut.

> *- Stephanie Morrill author of The Reinvention of Skylar Hoyt series and creator of www.GoTeenWriters.com*

Jan Christiansen will take you from blah to bingo, from yawn to yippee, and from alas to ah-ha! She knows how to kickstart your mind into full gear with witty expressions, clever anecdotes, and insightful plot elements. On those days when the ideas just don't seem to be flowing, Wake Up Your Muse is what this doctor prescribes.

> *- Dennis E. Hensley, Ph.D., author, How to Write What You Love and Make a Living at It*

Wake Up Your
MUSE

By Jan Christiansen

Illustrated by
Debbie Ridpath Ohi

WAKE UP YOUR MUSE

Published by Written World Communications
PO Box 26677
Colorado Springs, CO 80916
Writtenworldcommunications.com

Brought to you by the creative team at www.Written-World.com:
Kristine Pratt, Corinne Benes and Lynda K. Arndt

Library of Congress Cataloging-in-Publication Data
An Application to register this book for cataloging has been filed with the Library of Congress.
International Standard Book Number: 978-0-9829377-23

Cover image courtesy of iStockphotos.com
Cover design by Lynda K. Arndt

Interior images Copyright 2008-2011 by Debbie Ohi.
First appeared on www.willwriteforchocolate.com
Reprinted by permission of Curtis Brown, Ltd.

Printed in the United States of America

Introduction

As a writer there have been times I've sat staring at a blank page, unable to think of a single word to write. It's at those times I wonder if my "muse" is off somewhere taking a nap.

I know that an intriguing sentence or thought will get my creative juices flowing again. Unfortunately, my online searches for good writing prompts have proven frustrating.

I realized that if *I* needed creative prompts to jumpstart my writing, other writers must need them, too, and that's how *Wake Up Your Muse* was born.

With 1001 prompts, *Wake Up Your Muse* has enough ideas to keep you busy writing for a long time. In fact, using one prompt every day from *Wake Up Your Muse* will keep you writing for nearly three years!

For even more mileage, try switching the gender point of view in the prompts or choose different words for the *fill-in-the-blank* prompts. You might even try mixing and matching the prompts or combining two or more prompts together to spark an entirely different story. The possibilities are endless.

Visit us online at www.wakeupyourmuse.com.

Happy Writing!

Jan

Wake Up Your MUSE

1. The diver entered the hull of the ship through the gaping hole that had sunk her.

2. The warm pie cooling on the windowsill was too much temptation for the hungry boy.

3. He sat in his tent holding a flashlight and reading How to Survive a Bear Attack.

4. He grabbed the alarm clock and flung it across the room.

5. "Don't order the Blue Plate Special," whispered the waitress.

6. She insisted that the thermostat be lowered to 60 degrees.

7. He always hated that moment in their arguments when he realized he was wrong.

8. She quizzed me like she was emceeing a game show.

9. She scrunched up in a tiny ball, hoping that it would make her invisible.

10. The teacher hollered at me in front of the whole class.

11. She scampered around the room like a squirrel on the first day of hunting season.

12. He stared in the mirror, his image blurring before him, and wondered _____.

13. It was her first dinner with her fiancé's family and they served spaghetti.

14. A gnarly tree stood guard at the entrance of the cemetery.

15. It was hilarious—two grown women fighting over the last piece of fudge.

16. Her hands shook as she read her own birth certificate.

17. "I have to get off this couch!"

18. Trying to motivate her was like trying to start a fire with wet wood.

19. He couldn't see what he had because he was too focused on what he had lost.

20. I was prepared for anything she might say—except that.

21. I read about myself in chapter 2 of her autobiography.

22. She watched from her bedroom window as the birds held a skating party at the birdbath.

23. They were stunned when she admitted that she was on the ultimate form of birth control-abstinence.

24. Knee deep in dirty laundry, she wondered why _____.

25. She pounded out the words on the keyboard as if hitting the keys harder would convey the depths of her anger.

26. He found out quickly that girls don't like to be called buffalo butt.

27. She ducked behind the tree and held her breath.

28. The veins on the back of his hands looked like road maps.

29.   He mashed the gas pedal to the floor.

30.   She took one look at his bloody nose and burst out laughing.

31.   If she had known this was going to be her last meal, she would have ordered dessert.

32.   Why did he lie to her on the first day they met?

33.   When he arrived, her desk was in disarray and the phone was off the hook.

34.   She was tucking the baby in when she saw his face at the window.

35.   She didn't remember when, but she knew she had been in this room before.

36.   Was he really that hot or was it just his Mercedes that made him look that way?

37.   I wanted to slap the doctor across the face!

38.   She walked into the restaurant, looked around and suddenly remembered why she hated this place.

39.   She slammed on the brakes and time froze as the haunting song played on the radio.

40.   He wanted to stop her, to shut her up, but she just kept on laughing.

41.   The wind cut through her thin sweater like the briars were cutting through her legs, but she had to keep going.

42.   They ran the story on the front page of the newspaper. Now he would find her for sure.

43.   It was her face on the billboard, but she had never modeled for Victoria's Secret.

44.   She wondered how long she had been walking around with mustard on her chin.

45.   The dog snarled and refused to let her pass, but she had to reach the door.

And suddenly there it was, the perfect opening for Tommy's novel, lying at the bottom of his bowl of Alphabet Soup.

46.   I had only 24 hours left to _____.

47.   All she could see was a toe sticking out of the sand.

48.   She could hear him breathing, but she couldn't see him.

49.   In the blink of an eye, he went from zero to hero in her eyes.

50.   If only she hadn't missed his phone call, she would be sleeping in her own bed instead of this jail cell.

51.   She could hear the shower running, so she knew it was now or never.

52.   She looked hard at herself in the mirror, but this was not a face she recognized.

53.   After the funeral nothing mattered—until she found the note.

54.   She quit struggling and let herself go under for the final time.

55.   The elevator jerked to a stop, the lights flickered and five strangers were about to spend a very long night together.

56.   She dropped the note through the slot in his locker and wondered how he would feel about her once he knew the truth.

57.   It was a tempting offer, but could she trust him to keep his mouth shut?

58.   Why couldn't he see that they had to call off the wedding?

59.   I was wracking my brain trying to remember where I'd _____.

60.   She closed her eyes and tossed the coin into the fountain. If she had known that her wish would come true, she would have been more specific.

61.   "Your mother must have been mistaken," she lied.

62.   He was a great poker player, but he still couldn't tell if she was bluffing.

63.   She knew that Gladys would steal her prize-winning recipe if she left it on the table.

64.   His mama said you can't hurry love, but if he couldn't talk this girl into marrying him tonight, he would be dead by morning.

65.   She was sure she had been wearing her wedding ring before the party.

66.   She had stuck her nose into his business for the last time!

67.   "I've heard of borrowing a cup of sugar from a neighbor, but you want to borrow my what?"

68.   She didn't know she could fly until she was 5 years old.

69.   "Geez, could you warm those hands up a bit first?"

70. She was tired of being bullied by the good old boys. Now, it was her turn to make them cower.

71. He started down the aisle toward his seat when he noticed the lady in seat 23E pull a gun from her purse.

72. "Surprise!" they all yelled, then the room fell silent. The surprise was on them!

73. His wife had been calling him in sick for weeks but his secretary knew the truth.

74. At the end of the day, the only thing that really mattered was_____.

75. She was speechless. This was the same bracelet he'd given her for Christmas last year.

76. The cast on her leg made it impossible to run in the snow, but run she must—run or die.

77. The cookie jar his mother had given her shattered into a million pieces.

78. She had worked hard to lose those fifty pounds, but it hadn't made a bit of difference.

79. "I told you he's not here," she said, but I wasn't buying it.

80. She opened her locker and pulled the freshman out.

81. She looked around the cottage and thought, "It's the perfect place to fake my death.

82. I was at the end of my rope until _____.

83. She was grateful for the clouds covering the full moon as she dog-paddled her way across the lake and away from the cabin.

84. She whistled a happy tune as she added just a tiny pinch of arsenic to the batter.

85. She watched her fiance's son slip the merchandise into his pocket.

86. She intended to make the Olympics and no one—not even her mother—could stop her.

87. It was dangerous to be on the streets at night, but it was dangerous here at home, too.

88. He could reduce environmental pollution a lot if he just stopped eating beans!

89. She knew she shouldn't eavesdrop, but then, she never expected to hear them plotting her demise.

90. He took the keys and hid them in the freezer. She was too drunk to drive.

91. He pedaled faster, but the car continued to bear down on him.

92. He denied knowing her father, but something in his eyes told her he was lying.

93. He didn't believe in ghosts, but there she was, standing in the doorway.

94. She couldn't fall asleep. All she could think about was how different her life was going to be after tomorrow.

95. Sometimes it takes courage to walk away and today she was feeling very courageous.

96. She made us a fabulous wedding cake. Unfortunately _____.

97. "The early bird gets the worm," he said as he pulled the trigger.

98. She had hitched her wagon to a star, but she didn't realize he was a falling star.

99. She was up a creek without a paddle—literally!

100. Death by chocolate! What a delightful way to go.

101. The gray drizzle complimented her melancholy mood. A walk in the woods would be perfect.

102. She was tired of steamed vegetables. What she wanted was a good old-fashioned double hot fudge sundae!

103. Finally the old goat was retiring and I would be moving into the corner office. At least that's what I thought until he handed me my pink slip.

104. Working in a morgue, corpses didn't scare her, but this live one standing in front of her was terrifying.

105. He had skipped school to hang out on the beach with the guys. Now he wished he was sitting in Spanish class.

106. She opened her eyes and all she could see was light. "I thought blindness was supposed to be black," she thought.

107. Soft snowflakes began to fall. "How funny," she thought, "that winter should come on the very day my heart began to melt."

108. She watched from her bedroom window as the movers carried a coffin into the house next door.

109. She dialed his number for the seventh time that day, just to listen to his voice on the answering machine, but this time he picked up the phone.

110. I opened his school backpack and found a_____.

111. It worked. The babysitter was out cold!

112. He was supposed to be catching marlin in the Pacific, not tailing a cougar on the prowl in Beverly Hills.

113. She had waited all her life to see Paris. Bring on the romance!

114. She wove her way through the crowded streets, dodging the man that was following her.

115. With a crash, she shoved her shopping cart into mine.

116. "Fight!" someone yelled and everyone ran across the playground to watch the teachers duke it out.

117. She closed her eyes, made a wish and blew out all the candles. But when she opened her eyes, he was still there.

118. She placed the book back on the shelf, right where she had found it. No one must ever know she'd found the note hidden inside.

119. He watched her saunter by as if she didn't know him, as if she had never kissed him.

120. With the walls of the classroom closing in around her, she had to escape. She could not lose it in front of her students.

121. Mom sure had been acting funny lately.

122. The Junior Space Club built a receiver to see if they could detect signals from aliens. They were surprised to discover that it actually worked!

123. She opened the email from "eyes4U" and was shocked to see a picture of herself sleeping in her own bedroom. The time-stamp was midnight...last night!

124. As the car passed her, someone threw a briefcase out of the window.

125. She watched the food channel religiously, but the only thing she could really prepare well was _____ _____.

126. He hadn't planned to steal a car when he woke up this morning.

127. She pulled into Portland at 4:37 a.m., badly in need of a strong cup of coffee.

128. They rolled up their sleeping bags, tossed them in the back of the jeep and drove away from the freshly dug grave.

129. She was only one hour away from walking down the aisle.

130. The rash was spreading quickly.

131. He built her a tiny cabin in the woods, then locked her in it.

132. She hid the Bible in the folds of her skirt, then followed the guard into the work camp.

133. The letter from his brother read, "I've married your ex-wife."

134. Midway through Carlsbad Caverns the tour guide turned off the lights to demonstrate the utter darkness of the cave. He chose that moment to slip away from the crowd.

135. He could have made it into the Guinness Book of World Records with the number of lies he had told her.

136. She was just about to cloud up and rain all over him when he got down on one knee.

137. He knew the rule—no boys in the girl's locker room, but he had no choice.

138. She stared at the police sketch of the suspect. It was unmistakably her brother, but he had been with her last night.

139. This was truly a wedding gone horribly wrong, climaxed by the bride shoving her new mother-in-law face first into the cake.

140. She spread a blanket in the soft grass, laid down and fell promptly asleep. When she opened her eyes thirty minutes later, she found herself surrounded by hundreds of tiny fairies.

141. I wanted to pull the little snit right out of the drive-through window!

142. After the ceremony they surprised their guests by _____.

143. I was singing at the top of my lungs, so I didn't hear the siren until it was too late.

144. He awakened to the sound of the glass door on the balcony of his hotel room opening slowly.

145. They declared their never-ending love for one another at the foot of the Leaning Tower of Pisa, not knowing that they wouldn't see each other again for more than twenty years.

146. He had started the morning as just another tourist with a camera.

147. She stuffed the jewels into the sock monkey, and then carefully sewed up the seam.

148. "How hard is it to get an order right?" I asked. When the waitress rolled her eyes, I lost it.

149. She opened the wallet she'd found on the sidewalk and looked at the picture on the driver's license. Now, there was a guy she'd like to meet!

150. When the man of her dreams walked into her life her nightmare began.

151. She was a fast learner. She had already figured out how to get under his skin.

152. "I double-dog dare you," he said. I had no choice but to kiss the teacher.

153. The monitor read "Flight 2357- ON TIME"—the flight bringing her the child she had not seen since signing the adoption papers.

154. The sirens blared, the twister was bearing down. I stared it in the face and dared it to take me.

155. I'm smiling on the outside, but on the inside I'd like to
_____.

156. All she had to do was sign her name and her dreams would come true. So why was she hesitating?

157. I had been totally stoked about starting college until my mother announced that she had also enrolled at Ohio State.

158. He couldn't believe his eyes. The cells were mutating at an alarming rate!

159. He was sure her voice could rip a hole right through the space-time continuum.

160. She thought drinking was cool until she barfed all over the cutest guy in school.

161. Was this the real thing or just a clever counterfeit?

162. He leaned forward in his chair, raised a crooked finger to my face and said, "_____."

163. The car full of jokers pulled up to the drive through for the fourth time that night, but this time she was ready for them.

164. Looking around the room, she felt like she had just stepped 100 years back in time.

165. It had only been six months and already he was feeling the itch to move on.

166. His horse knew the way home, but the cowboy should have known better than to fall asleep in the saddle.

167. He showed the boy again how to tie a hook onto the fishing line.

168. She went back out to bring in the rest of the groceries and came face to face with a stranger holding the last two bags, a gallon of milk and a gun.

169. For once she had shut the class full of hoodlums up, but she was pretty sure she would be fired for what she had written on the blackboard.

170. His gnarled fingers were surprisingly soft as they stroked my cheek.

171. They had stirred the sleeping warrior in him when they laid their hands on his wife.

172. I couldn't believe they were going to pay me $100,000 to _____.

173. She fell backwards into the pool and allowed her body to go limp. Could she hold her breath long enough to make him think she was dead?

174. "You could put an eye out like that," he thought. He would have laughed out loud were it not for the searing pain in his right pupil.

175. He leaned against the lamppost trying to remember what city he was in.

176. He was forever 21 in her mind, just as he was in the picture she held in her hand.

177. In a different time, a different place, this might have worked.

178.   Peanut butter, jelly and a loaf of bread. That should last him a week.

179.   She didn't believe in hypnosis, still...

180.   She licked the spoon as she watched Grandma put the cake into the oven.

181.   The toe of my shoe got caught in the escalator.

182.   She discreetly placed the book on the table in the food court, then walked away.

183.   He dialed the number and watched from a distance as she answered her cell phone.

184.   "Experience Mexico" the sign said. Oh, he was experiencing Mexico all right.

185.   He hadn't heard from his college buddy in years.

186.   He had been volunteering at the senior center for years without anyone suspecting a thing.

187.   The simple lie I'd told when I was 12 years old had caused all this turmoil.

URL: www.willwriteforchocolate.com

WILL WRITE FOR CHOCOLATE   Copyright©2008 Debbie Ridpath Ohi

188.   Walking down this hall brought back a thousand memories.

189.   He looked at the tree. It was much bigger than he remembered, but this was the tree.

190.   I had been teased one too many times.

191.   There's a place deep within where love and hatred are born.

192.   She was forgetting things—not just where she left her car keys, but names, places and events.

193.   Once his presidency was over, he thought his family would be safe.

194.   The girls giggled, then ran off, leaving him covered in _____.

195.   She loved being his daughter, except for when he was drunk.

196.   The article was meant to expose an injustice, not get her arrested.

197.   "Your lips are saying one thing, but your eyes are telling a whole different story."

198.   When it comes to love, some men are general practitioners and some are skilled specialists.

199.   My heart has lied to me a thousand times, so why should I listen to it now?

200.   Eloquent slander cuts just as deep as common gossip.

201.   She was standing way too close.

202.   It had been dead silent in our house for days.

203.   I may have been named after him, but I refused to be like him.

204.   He took the steps two at a time, clutching the envelope tightly.

205.   A whole summer at Grandma's—this would either be the best vacation ever, or the worst.

206.   The bushy-haired stranger leaned over and kissed my wife.

207. She could feel her heart pounding erratically as her throat began to tighten.

208. He lay staring up at the ceiling fan, wondering _____.

209. I closed my eyes for just a moment and when I opened them again, nothing looked familiar.

210. The beach was deserted—just the way she liked it for her early morning run.

211. He drained the bottle, lit another cigarette and waited.

212. The cabbie looked vaguely familiar.

213. The old bookstore had that musty smell she loved.

214. The roads were slippery and his intentions were evil.

215. The pipes groaned, then vomited rusty water out into the sink.

216. She crossed the finish line, exhausted and happy, but dead last.

217. They had planted the bug deep inside his brain, now they could monitor his every thought.

218. He sat on the cold floor, wrapped in a blanket.

219. They met every morning at the same coffeehouse, shared the same table, talked for thirty minutes before going their separate ways to work. And she still didn't know his name.

220. She strapped the baby to her back, picked up the basket of fruit and headed for the market.

221. A great basketball coach does not a good birthing coach make.

222. She had a three-course dinner; a diet pill, a diuretic and a laxative.

223. "Let's go, princess," said the cop.

224. He woke up in a pool of sweat.

225. "You're not one of us anymore," she said.

226. I saw her stealing money out of my tip jar.

227. He had no qualms about hitting on an engaged woman.

228. "Well, now you know," she said, placing the ring in his hand.

229. She waded into the muddy water.

230. "This is going to take awhile," he said.

231. The operation was successful, but weeks later _____.

232. "I've been having these awful dreams."

233. "I know you're not sorry, but you're going to be if you don't sign this."

234. You would not have noticed him if you had passed him in the hall or sat at the same table with him in the cafeteria.

235. They packed her frail body in ice and prayed for the fever to break.

236. He sat hunched over in the saddle, rain dripping from the brim of his hat and blood dripping from the hole in his side.

237. The train steamed through the countryside, carrying her back to the place she had escaped from so long ago.

238. He shoved a few things into a suitcase, dropped it out the window, and then jumped out himself.

239. The boys headed into the wilderness carrying their backpacks and a hunger for adventure.

240. She had learned to live with fear, but could she live with the truth?

241. She turned her head as they wheeled his body away, a little smile playing on her lips.

242. The phone rang just as she was sinking into a tub full of bubbles.

243. Love was coming at him like a runaway locomotive.

244. The work conditions were deplorable, but they had no choice. If they didn't work, they couldn't pay for the operation.

245. "You have extraordinary powers of perception," she said sarcastically.

246. She lifted the beaters from the bowl and cake batter splattered all over everything.

247. Hey, I'm no Superman, but I couldn't just sit by and watch _____.

248. She ran through the cornfield, ignoring the sharp blades cutting into her bare arms.

249. They posed for the annual faculty picture. Thirty-seven teachers— one of them a murderer.

250. He stood on the balcony of his studio apartment staring out at Lake Michigan.

251. She took an abnormal interest in the type of work I do.

252. She had an aquatic look about her.

253. She dipped the chicken in boilin' water and commenced to pluckin' it.

254. He had already made several clumsy attempts at proposing, so she just up and popped the question herself.

255. He said that after the wallpaper was changed it would be a very nice bedroom, except for the bars on the windows.

256. Sunlight filtered through the sheer curtains as they blew softly in the breeze at the open window.

257. The girl in the hooded sweatshirt slipped through the fence and _____.

258. The old man and woman looked like they were in a foot race—she with her walker and he with his cane.

259. The deputy rubbed the back of his neck and wondered how he was going to write this one up.

260. He grabbed the sticky black receiver and dropped a quarter in the slot.

261. They sat glaring at one another across the candlelit table.

262. "What do you mean it's not about me?" she asked.

263. He leaned over and spoke into her good ear.

264. She found a gift-wrapped box on her desk when she returned from lunch.

265. I saw him headed for a heartache, but couldn't bring myself to tell him how I knew.

266. I scoured the newspaper for three days, but the story never showed. I began to relax.

267. The couple next to me argued throughout the entire flight. So much for flying the friendly skies.

268. He was stopped at a red light when the old woman opened his passenger door and got in.

269. Yesterday she enjoyed the spice markets of Mumbai, this morning she had taken her first elephant ride and tonight she found herself stuffed in the trunk of a car.

270. The last three days of my life sounded like something out of a paperback novel.

271. She rummaged around in the attic until she found it.

272. "This will only hurt for a minute, Mr. Watts," said the nurse. Then she stuck him with the needle before he could tell her that his name was Stephens, not Watts.

273. I opened the closet door just a crack and watched him search the room.

274.   She packed her bags and ran away. Nobody was going to put her in a nursing home!

275.   The wagon wheels bounced in and out of the ruts in the road, jostling the _____.

276.   The screen door slammed behind the kids for the umpteenth time today.

277.   My mother sat sprawled in the middle of the sidewalk, her roller skate wheels still spinning.

278.   I breathed deep the fragrance of spring lilacs and wondered if I would ever return to this place.

279.   It was the first night in their new home and it was also their last night in their new home.

280.   His mother's wedding dress was beautiful, but I only had two weeks left to fit into it.

281.   He paced his cell trying to sort out the events that had landed him in prison.

282.   They say there are no snakes in Ireland, but after her encounter with Shamus O'Malley, she could certainly dispute that point.

283.   She had to get help immediately, but the storm had knocked out the phone lines.

284.   He was absorbed in deep thought when she slipped up behind him.

285.   She couldn't believe her eyes. Their engagement rings were identical!

286.   If only I had kept driving when I saw the lady with the broken down Chevy and gorgeous legs.

287.   She peeled the aged paper from the back of the picture she had bought at the yard sale.

288.   She was ready to be his wife, but first, he must know the truth.

Will Write For Chocolate URL: WillWriteForChocolate.com

Hi Michael! Where were you?

Checking out the big new bookstore on Bloor Street.

It's very shiny, and it seems to only have three categories of books for young people.

Really? Which ones?

Picture Books, Middle Grade, and Vampire.

Thanks to Amber Lough! Copyright©2009 Debbie Ridpath Ohi comics@me.com

289.   Bobby wondered how long a first kiss should be.

290.   If they had known her at all, they would have picked another victim.

291.   The jack slipped, leaving him pinned under the car.

292.   She said those four dreaded words, "We need to talk."

293.   He certainly knew his way around a kitchen.

294.   I saw her two aisles over, squeezing the melons.

295.   I should have listened to my best friend when he tried to warn me about _____.

296.   He knew he was in the doghouse, but the least she could do was throw him a bone.

297.   He watched the old 45 spin on the turntable and thought back to the night they had danced to this song.

298.   If she wouldn't give him custody of the dog, he would just have to kidnap it.

299.   He had hiked these mountains a hundred times, but he had never noticed that cave before.

300. From her bedroom window she could clearly see her neighbor digging in his back yard.

301. He checked his watch for the third time. If she didn't get back soon, he was going to leave her there.

302. She opened the old shoebox and pulled out the letters she had hidden from her husband for so long.

303. Last night I finally told her I loved her. It was the last words she ever heard.

304. The air hung heavy in the small room. Even the light streaming through the window couldn't brighten the atmosphere.

305. Volunteering to work in the school cafeteria was ingenious. Now he could _____.

306. I'd like to think there's a reason for everything, but this just didn't make sense.

307. The door closed behind me and I began to panic.

308. Tired of waiting, I took matters into my own hands.

309. Jumping out of the limo was a risk, but it was one worth taking.

310. He kissed her goodbye at the top of the ski slope, just in case..

311. There's massive potential for failure here, I thought.

312. The room was filled with a strangely familiar scent.

313. I had heard about desperate housewives, but never thought I'd be one!

314. He looked at his watch, shook my hand and took off running.

315. It was a small investment with a huge return.

316. I wanted to tell them how I really felt. Instead, I smiled and made small talk.

317. This was a shotgun wedding with a real twist!

318. "We're running out of time," she whispered.

319. He hated going to the doctor anyway, but this was going to be downright embarrassing.

320. "I think we're making progress," she said with a twinkle in her eye.

321. I asked her to keep it simple, but once again, she went way overboard.

322. I never panic in a crisis, but there's a first time for everything.

323. He felt the tire blow and struggled to maintain control of the bus.

324. My grandma was not your typical grandmother.

325. The bus was crowded, standing room only, when suddenly _____.

326. Every man in the room gravitated toward the blonde in the red dress.

327. She laid all her cards on the table.

328. Normally, I thrived on competition, but this time I knew I didn't stand a chance.

329. I thought it was all too good to be true. Ten minutes later I found I was right.

330. She hid in the closet of her dorm room, not daring to breathe.

331. I could tell by the smile on his face that he had not yet heard the news.

332. I have to admit that I like explosions.

333. It was a good plan, gone horribly wrong.

334. The wide-open spaces made this Los Angeles girl afraid she would be swallowed up in the vastness of Montana.

335. "You've been eliminated," she said.

336. I opened the door to what had obviously been the nursery.

337. He threw the instruction manual across the room.

338. He kept shooting the glass bulbs off the Christmas tree.

339. She waved good-bye and boarded the plane bound for _____.

340. It was the night of my sixteenth birthday.

341. It was the most fun I ever had in a car.

342. The pounding rhythm of the drums suddenly stopped.

343. She stumbled backward and fell right into a cactus patch.

344. I could feel myself slipping.

345. He was on a dangerous mission—return with the wrong brand and she would have his head.

346. She was desperate to unravel the secrets of her past.

347. He shimmied out to the end of the limb and dropped into the neighbor's back yard.

348. Tonight, she was enjoying the limelight, but she knew that tomorrow morning she would regret every word she was saying.

349. Her agent promised her fame and fortune, but how she was going to achieve that playing a talking carrot was beyond her.

350. She could handle men, but this little, bitty boy was too much for her.

351. He was amused by the way she stared at the lobster tail as if an alien had been boiled and set before her.

352. I was mortified when my cell phone rang right in the middle of _____.

353. A somber mood hung over the room.

354. Was it a look-alike or was this really the President of the United States sitting beside him?

355. He turned down the secluded road and flipped off his headlights.

356. She took one look at him and the words lounge lizard popped into her head.

357. The lullaby sounded hauntingly familiar and out of place.

358. She slept with a machete under the mattress.

359. She wore the macaroni necklace proudly into the business meeting.

360. The sound of him grinding his teeth was driving her mad.

361. He said it was just my inner child crying for attention. Right now my inner child just wanted to kick him in the shins.

362. Sammy sold apples and oranges on the corner, but an extra fiver would get you a carton of black market cigarettes.

363. I don't believe in sea monsters, but it's only my third day into the cruise and this guy just might qualify.

364. She had come to Alaska because she heard that the ratio of men to women would practically guarantee her chances of meeting Mr. Right.

365. Mother said a prayer of thanksgiving, just as she did every year on the first day of school.

366. The freckle-faced 5-year-old sat on the park bench eating an ice cream cone.

367. That little yapping mutt she calls Poopsy could very well be the deal-breaker in our relationship.

368. What management called a fun, interactive personality test had just cost me a promotion.

369. She decided to break the tension by announcing her pregnancy.

370. I had stumbled onto something big and it was evident that somebody wanted to shut me up.

371. The twins were used to switching places to fool people, but this time _____.

372. We stepped ashore in Ireland, not knowing what the future held.

373. He held out a cupcake topped with fluffy pink frosting and a lone flickering candle. Nestled in the pink frosting was a sparkling diamond ring.

374. The building shook as the train carrying commuters into the city passed her tiny apartment.

375. It was the most widely known best-kept secret in our little town.

376. She collected men like she collected handbags.

377. He tried to give her the brush-off, but she wasn't going anywhere.

378. She tilted her head back, threw her hands in the air and laughed as her bike careened down the hill.

379. She took one look at the handsome doctor and vowed never to eat apples again.

380. She always took a minute to bow her head and thank God before a meal, but what she didn't know was that praying in public was illegal in this country.

381. This was no itsy-bitsy spider climbing up the water spout; it was a huge tarantula climbing up her pant leg.

382. She'd heard of the lazy days of summer, but if he didn't get off that sofa and do something she was going to clobber him.

383. She sat cross-legged on the floor with her eyes closed, her serene exterior masking the raging storm within.

384. The painting looked so real, I had to lean in for a closer look. That was when _____.

385. We ate day-old bread torn into chunks and covered with milk and sugar.

386. He clocked in at precisely 8:59 a.m. every morning and clocked out at exactly 5:01 p.m. each evening.

387. She discovered the perfect cure for PMS—shopping!

388. She thought the job interview had gone well until she stood to leave, tripped over her own feet and fell flat on her face.

389. She was headed for Hollywood and stardom, but got sidetracked by a handsome cowboy in Colorado.

390. Her lemon raspberry cream pie was a delightful but deadly delectation.

391. When she received threatening notes in the mail, she laughed it off, but when she found one in her coat pocket, she stopped laughing.

392. I discovered that my adoption had taken place under shady circumstances.

393. She arrived in Hollywood prepared to struggle for years before becoming a rich and famous actress. She was not prepared to become an overnight sensation.

394. My computer had crashed, the phones were dead and the elevator was out of order. I had no choice but to take the stairs.

395. When my finger touched the delicate features of the painting, I felt myself being pulled into the scene on the canvas.

396. He had discovered her secret. Should he tell her or let her go on believing that he didn't know?

397. Running barefoot through the tall green grass had felt so good until _____.

398. He was flashy and full of adventure, so what did he want with a mousy little thing like her?

399. His lectures left the students on the edge of their seats and begging for more.

400. She was the new kid on the block and already she had stolen my two best friends.

401. It paid to make friends with the school janitor!

402. She didn't know how to answer his questions without compromising her cover.

403. He flew over the handlebars and landed smack dab in the middle of the old man's prize rose bushes.

404. He paced the hospital hallway praying for a miracle, even though he didn't believe in them.

405. The frown on her face and the wrinkles on her forehead told me I was in big trouble.

406. She slipped on her robe and headed to the kitchen for her morning coffee.

407. The huge lump in his throat made it hard to swallow.

408. He erased the word so vigorously that it made a hole in the paper.

409. She opened her dresser drawer and perused her stash of forbidden candy.

Will Write For Chocolate   Copyright©2006 Debbie Ridpath Ohi

27

410.   "I should be home in time for dinner," he said, but they both knew he was lying.

411.   The last thing she remembered was her birthday party in the penthouse.

412.   He climbed up on the lunch table and yelled, "I love this girl and I don't care who knows it!"

413.   I curled up in the cardboard box at the end of the alley.

414.   The plan was simple—get in and get out, until _____.

415.   The night closed in and the darkness threatened to swallow them up as they floated down the crocodile infested river.

416.   Someone had clipped huge chunks of fur from her prized poodle just minutes before the dog show was scheduled to begin.

417.   She was addicted but not to drugs, alcohol or cigarettes. She was addicted to crafting and she needed an intervention!

418.   The cat left a trail of bloody paw prints across the wooden floor.

419.   She chewed all five sticks of gum, then patched the hole in the radiator with the gooey glob.

420.   He ignored the thorns scratching his arms and legs. His mind was on the blackberry cobbler Mom had promised to make.

421.   She brushed aside the cobwebs and opened the cellar door.

422.   Why did dating him remind her of hand-to-hand combat?

423.   He looked like he was having a seizure right in the middle of the dance floor.

424.   The pressure cooker hissed violently then blew its top.

425.   Just his luck. He sets one foot on the beach and a seagull drops a bomb on his head.

426.   The door to the stall wouldn't open no matter how hard she pushed.

427. She felt like she was back in grade school, chasing boys on the playground.

428. He woke to the smell of flapjacks and sausages sizzling on the griddle.

429. She thought he was just another gringo wanting more than a drink for his two bits.

430. If she juggled her grocery money just right, she could squirrel away enough by Christmas to buy a bus ticket out of this one-horse town.

431. The hair-netted cafeteria lady plopped a big spoonful of unidentifiable gruel on his plate, then grunted at him to move on.

432. He gazed up at a fingernail moon, enjoying the coyote concert in the distance.

433. It was just a friendly hug, wasn't it?

434. He felt the truck hydroplane.

435. This was her fourth ice cream sandwich in a row. She was out of control and all because _____.

436. The county fair—sausage and pepper sandwiches, funnel cakes, cotton candy, corn dogs and ice cream on a stick, followed by a ride on the Tilt-A-Whirl.

437. The Old West ghost town was an unlikely hideout for a modern-day cyber thief.

438. Insanity was the perfect disguise for this undercover investigation.

439. This quaint bed and breakfast held the secret to her past, but someone did not want her to uncover that secret.

440. She was an unwelcome interruption in his busy day.

441. He remembered the hearty jambalaya his Creole mother had made and wondered if his new bride would get upset if he suggested she call for the recipe.

442. They were unlikely partners in crime.

443. He was a jackass, but he was her jackass.

444. He dropped a dime in the jukebox and selected B3, then stepped onto the dance floor and did a perfect waltz with an imaginary partner.

445. She was juggling three men—her son, her husband and her father, and they all wanted something different from her.

446. He lifted the jug to his lips and began to blow as Mama strummed the banjo.

447. She sat on the veranda sipping her mint julep, a loaded shotgun cradled in her arms.

448. He was just one keystroke away from embezzling a million dollars.

449. Her face flushed with anger and her fingers curled in to make a fist.

450. He raced up the stairs two at a time.

451. She jabbed her bony finger into my chest.

452. They couldn't believe their father was actually going to marry this

_____

453. If her goal was to destroy his round of golf, she was doing a good job.

454. His uniform had to be really clean for the big game, so he used a double-dose of detergent

455. His fear of commitment was so great, he couldn't even pick out a box of cereal for himself.

456. She had had the hiccups for five days straight.

457. She considered herself a serious journalist for people with inquiring minds.

458. He positioned the ladder directly below her window.

459.   "Why did you hang up on me?"

460.   They had only met once, but it was a meeting neither would ever forget.

461.   The snowman began to melt, exposing the body.

462.   I hid behind the curtain and watched her as she passed by.

463.   She despised the way he talked down to her.

464.   I knew it was just my imagination, but I couldn't shake the feeling that I was being watched.

465.   She skillfully evaded my question.

466.   The tree house was a great place to spend a summer afternoon.

467.   He found a partial phone number scribbled on the yellow legal pad.

468.   While the storm raged outside, she poured herself a cup of hot tea and sank into a comfy chair to finish her book.

469.   His plane was delayed, forcing him to spend the night at the airport.

470.   An awful smell emanated from the smoking toaster.

471.   He was always so even tempered that it took her by surprise when he slammed his fist on the table.

472.   A canister of tear gas shot through the window and landed at my feet.

473.   She stared at her reflection in the silver teaspoon.

474.   I could hear my mother calling my name, but I couldn't answer because _____.

475.   He stepped out of the saloon into the dusty streets of Tombstone and walked slowly toward the OK Corral, imagining that he was Wyatt Earp.

476. He spit the tooth out into his hand and started laughing.

477. "She's dead to me," he said.

478. She emerged from the tent holding a baby.

479. He swung the telescope around and aimed it at the doorway across the street.

480. He drew back, intending to slap her in the face.

481. I was tempted to just pick it up and walk away.

482. A single tear rolled down his cheek.

483. It was just a temporary arrangement, but I hoped that it would become permanent.

484. She had made up her mind and there was nothing I could do to change it.

485. She looked him directly in the eye as she gave her testimony.

486. She pointed her car toward Amarillo, hit the gas and never looked back.

487. It should have been an open and shut case, but I was falling in love with the primary suspect.

488. Three years of therapy had not done as much for me as had the last thirty minutes.

489. He was too thick-headed to realize what she was trying to say.

490. The thermometer read 114.5—impossible!

491. I could hear the unmistakable sounds of a candy bar being unwrapped in the dark.

492. He felt a sharp pain in his thigh.

493. Even the sound of her flip-flops was annoying me today.

494. She thumped the boy's head sharply with her thimbled finger.

495. He called it his thingamabob and took it with him wherever he went.

496. If she had a magic wand right now, she'd use it to _____.

497. The air was thick with accusations.

498. The deal had gone perfectly and now he could relax and enjoy his last few days in Tokyo. Then the phone rang and everything changed.

499. Thirteen was an awful age to be in love.

500. The wind was picking up and thunderheads were forming to the north. We had to hurry.

501. He was going to throttle that boy!

502. She had no choice but to break her promise.

503. She refused to believe that she was just plain white trash.

504. She loosened the final screw and escaped through the skylight.

505. This had been a dream come true, but now it was time to wake up.

506. The strange image scrawled on the wall sparked a long forgotten memory.

507. He refused to part with the threadbare flowered sofa.

508. The thinly veiled threat was meant to scare her off.

509. They were partnered in the three-legged race.

510. She pounded on the landlord's door with a wrench.

511. It was a standoff between the skunk and the determined boy.

512. He spent his sixteenth summer working in a slaughterhouse.

513. She pretended to be sleepwalking.

514. He put a thick slab of bacon between two pieces of bread.

515. Mother delivered her own emancipation proclamation, leaving the six of us to fend for ourselves all summer.

516. "Cut me some slack," he said.

517. The slander was meant to discredit her, but instead it had earned her a promotion.

518. It was the third time this week that she had been late to work because of _____.

519. My grandma was slaphappy.

520. Impeccably dressed, she looked totally out of place in this sleazy hotel.

521. He zipped himself into his sleeping bag and put out the lantern.

522. She swung the sledgehammer again; this time it hit the windshield.

523. The mountain road was icing over, but there was nowhere for them to stop for the night.

524. They arrested every girl who had attended the slumber party.

URL: www.willwriteforchocolate.com

WILL WRITE FOR CHOCOLATE   Copyright©2008 Debbie Ridpath Ohi

525. She aimed the sled directly at his ankles and hoped he wouldn't turn around.

526. He inched his way along the wall, trying to see through the blackness.

527. Her feet slid out from under her and she landed flat on her derriere.

528. She wanted to slap that silly grin right off his face.

529. He followed the stream for several miles, and then turned inward through the forest.

530. It was an embarrassing slippage, to be sure.

531. The agent walked her through the house, pointing out all the features, but he intentionally left out its infamous history.

532. He trudged through the slush dragging his backpack behind him.

533. The boy opened his eyes for the first time in weeks when the puppy licked his face.

534. He floated down the river, scanning the shoreline for a good place to hide.

535. He covered his stained t-shirt with a clean smock and went back to work.

536. He passed the pack around and we all choked our way through our first cigarette.

537. Not caring what anyone in the office thought, she turned up the radio and belted out her favorite song.

538. It was only Monday and already the teacher was glaring at us.

539. He pushed up the window, slipped over the sill and hit the ground running.

540. She heard a sniffle coming from behind the overstuffed chair.

541. He had been snookered by a blue-eyed angel in high heels.

542. She closed her eyes and tried to remember why she had stopped
_____.

543. It was Christmas snow—magic snow.

544. She expected me to brush my teeth, comb my hair and wash my hands every single day.

545. He emptied the entire bottle of dishwashing liquid into the fountain.

546. His social worker labeled him incorrigible, but I found him to be a delightful challenge.

547. She showed up at the church social a bit tipsy.

548. I had inherited my father's penchant for adventure.

549. As her eyes pierced mine, I felt like I had been injected with truth serum.

550. He sang his song and I felt totally exposed to the world.

551. Lesson #1: Never mimic your mama when she's mad.

552. The housekeeper saw everything, but said nothing.

553. She threw on a sweatshirt and jeans, pulled on her boots and ran out to the barn.

554. A clump of trees practically hid the car from those driving by.

555. He stood on shaky legs and made his way across the ice.

556. I was so busy carrying on an imaginary conversation with my father that I didn't notice when he walked into the room.

557. She stood motionless as the hummingbirds flitted all around her.

558. She felt the sting and knew she had only minutes to inject herself.

559. A month ago he had been a down-and-outer.

560. Next thing I know, this woman throws herself into my arms and begs me to protect her.

561. Her pickles won the blue ribbon every year. Who would have thought that _____..

562. It didn't take a psychic to figure out where she was going with this.

563. I pried the lid off the box with a crowbar.

564. I had all the proof I needed to clear my name.

565. The propane tank exploded.

566. He had been promising to fix the stairs for months.

567. The sign on the door said private, but he didn't let that stop him.

568. They smuggled the goods down the Ohio River.

569. An oily substance covered my steering wheel.

570. I felt the tentacles wrap around my right leg.

571. He climbed twenty feet up into the old oak tree and refused to come down.

572. I didn't know I had an uncle until I read the obituary.

573. The house had not been occupied for twelve years, so why was the phone still connected?

574. I first saw her lying under a flowering dogwood.

575. He scrutinized my every move.

576. The scuttlebutt around the office was that he had a gambling habit.

577. She hollowed out the walnut shell, hid the diamond inside and glued the halves back together.

578. She let her mind wander down that well-traveled path

579. All she had to do was hit the button and within thirty seconds
     _____.

580. It was a fluke really, that he happened to pass by at that moment.

581. He crushed the flower in his hand, and then let it drop to the
     ground.

582. I never suspected that she was secretly preparing my demise.

583. He could write The Idiot's Guide to Sticking Your Foot in Your
     Mouth.

584. The foliage was thick enough to conceal her while providing the
     perfect vantage point.

585. He carefully folded the map and stuck it back in his pocket.

586. It was a foolhardy thing to do.

587. He lost his footing on the slippery rock and plunged twenty feet
     downward.

588. The sticky fly strip hanging from the ceiling was full of fly corpses.

589. The foreman cut corners and pocketed the extra money.

590. Closing her eyes while her feet soaked, she eavesdropped on the
     conversation of the women next to her.

591. He frequented Jerry's Java Hut, but not for the coffee.

592. She was not familiar with medical jargon. Was a hematoma fatal?

593. Even with her jaw wired shut, she managed to harp at him nonstop.

594. She smiled as he slathered the hot bread with butter and strawberry
     jam.

595. Her eyes narrowed and her lips curled into a thin, tight smile.

596. The minute we crossed the border into Canada, I began to breathe
     easy.

597. He flipped upside down on the monkey bars, lost his grip and dropped to the ground.

598. By the end of the day, the rumor had spread through the entire office.

599. She tried to picture him without the mustache and beard.

600. The necklace was beautiful, but she refused it because she knew _____.

601. She calmly folded her napkin, stood, dropped her engagement ring into his water glass and walked away.

602. They asked him to go undercover and infiltrate the Boy Scouts of America.

603. The way he sucks up to the boss nauseates me.

604. She frosted thirty-six cupcakes, then topped them with multi-colored sprinkles.

605. They issued a nationwide alert for the fugitives and their foreign hostage.

606. A gust of wind ripped the tree up by its roots and sent it crashing through the roof of the little schoolhouse.

607. The old hag refused to tell him where she had hidden the key.

608. Her delicate porcelain hands performed the ancient Chinese tea ritual. Who would have believed those slender fingers could render a man lifeless with one quick jab to the thorax?

609. He fixed the crosshairs on the woodpecker and pulled the trigger.

610. He hid in the cupola until nightfall.

611. She had a strict curfew and a snitch for a little brother.

612. She knew it was the custom to remove one's shoes, but what if you had a terrible foot odor?

613. The judge ordered joint custody, but she had no intentions of complying with that order.

614. Suddenly I understood what she had been trying to tell me over the phone.

615. All he wanted was an ego massage.

616. I thought past experience had made me immune to her venomous charm.

617. The extended forecast called for good weather outside, but a storm was brewing inside our vacation cabin.

618. Beads of sweat ran down his back as he strained to _____.

619. She added just a touch of vanilla extract to the hot tea to disguise the taste of the sedative.

620. Only when he attempted to remove the hook, did he discover that northern pike have sharp teeth.

621. She rubbed the soft flannel of her grandfather's shirt and knew this is how she would always remember him.

622. The old fleabag turned out to be my best friend after all.

623. The neighborhood had an eclectic flavor

624. I reached over the seat and took his bag of popcorn just as the lights went down in the theater.

625. The flood waters were rising, but we couldn't evacuate with her in this condition.

626. Claustrophobia seized him by the throat as the horde of autograph seekers closed in.

627. He soothed the restless herd with a lonesome tune on his harmonica.

628. She would rather spend the night in her car than to call him for help.

629.   He thought he'd give himself a hernia carrying her over the threshold.

630.   She turned the corner just in time to see _____.

631.   The high-level security precautions were no match for her persuasive skills.

632.   He refused to believe the indisputable evidence of her guilt.

633.   She was so desperate that she popped an extra hormone pill.

634.   The house was quiet, too quiet.

635.   She thought it harmless gossip until someone turned up dead.

636.   He fiddled with the dial on the radio searching for just the right mood music.

637.   He intended to accomplish his New Year's resolution before the night was out.

638.   A revival broke out in the most crime-ridden part of town.

639.   She reworked the truth until it suited her purposes.

640.   He did an about-face and walked away from the only woman he had ever loved.

641. She sat in the waiting room, wondering if she could really go through with it.

642. He looked at the crowd and saw a thousand pockets just ripe for the picking.

643. His morning ritual was interrupted by a disturbing phone call.

644. They had been rivals for years, but now they must join forces in order to survive.

645. Only he would think a ceramic owl bought at a roadside stand would make a romantic anniversary gift.

646. "Oh, sassafras," she said, which was as close as she ever got to cussing.

647. He eased the bush-plane onto the faint tracks that served as a runway.

648. She jiggled the latch on the rolltop desk until she heard a click.

649. The stained-glass windows cast eerie shadows across the sanctuary.

650. She quickly tied her apron strings, mussed her hair and answered the door.

651. What kind of sicko would bury a body in a sandbox?

652. She had an invitation, but he couldn't find her name anywhere on the guest list.

653. She fingered the ivory rosette broach.

654. He immersed himself in the sights, sounds and culture of Appalachia.

655. The sheets felt like sandpaper on his sunburned skin.

656. She unwrapped her sandwich and fed it to the pigeons.

657. It had been thirty years since she had seen him. Would he still think _____.

658.   The little town was saturated with bigotry.

659.   He placed the valise in the airport locker and walked away.

660.   They said it was a case of spontaneous combustion.

661.   She smeared petroleum jelly on the toilet seat.

662.   He lifted her veil and gave her a cool kiss on the cheek.

663.   His voice was smooth as Black Velvet and just as intoxicating.

664.   She struggled to the surface and fought to catch her breath before being dragged back under.

665.   She felt like a ventriloquist's dummy.

666.   He downed his sarsaparilla, wiped his mouth on his sleeve and stepped into the street for the showdown.

667.   The autopsy proved that he was not murdered, but I knew I had killed him.

668.   Her jet-black hair, tattooed body and rough talk were a cover-up for the scared little girl inside.

669.   The simple description in her personal ad didn't do her justice.

670.   "Step away from the box of doughnuts, Mom," said her son, but he was nowhere in sight.

671.   He stumbled through the door of the police station.

672.   He was thoroughly confused by her illogical behavior.

673.   Being deaf certainly had its advantages.

674.   She slipped the memory card from her camera to him.

675.   He popped another cough drop into his mouth, but it didn't help.

676.   If she could only convince him to loan her $10,000, she could _____.

677. She stared at the image in the ornate oval frame.

678. He slipped a business card into the director's pocket.

679. The boy and his dog chased the waves back into the ocean.

680. She spritzed on the most expensive perfume sample at the cosmetic counter.

681. "You're supposed to remove the beaters from the mixer before you lick them," she said.

682. Her woman's intuition raised all kinds of red flags.

683. By his calculations, they should arrive in three days if the winds blew steady.

684. She snatched her underwear from the clothesline.

685. If she didn't turn that treadmill off soon, he was going to go upstairs and pound on her door.

686. He poured the jar of change out onto his bed.

687. She read the letter again, unwilling to accept what her sister had written.

688. She pulled away from the gas station with the pump nozzle and hose trailing from her car's tank.

689. Jill had hated him since the day he _____.

690. Pain shot up my leg as her cleats dug into my calf.

691. If he hadn't been so slow, he would have figured out that she was just using him.

692. What he wanted to say was, "Yes, that dress does make you look fat!"

693. He opened his car door just as the biker squeezing between lanes of traffic got to him.

694. It was a fairy house made of twigs and moss and nestled at the base of a giant oak.

695. He had built a series of secret passages that allowed him to move from apartment to apartment undetected.

696. Before he started reading a new book, he always turned to page 17 and read the third sentence on the page.

697. It's true; dogs do get brain freeze if they eat ice cream too fast.

698. She tilted her face to the sky and let the rain mingle with her tears.

699. The bistro served the worst food in town, but the cutest girl in town served it.

700. Ten years later, she pulled the torn dress from her closet and put it on.

701. He had accidentally shot his best coon dog.

702. That was my first encounter with blackmail.

703. He sprinkled the rose with sneezing powder.

704. He took the blame, even though he knew who had really caused the fire.

705. She helped herself to the contents of his bank account.

706. An unnatural fog rolled in from the bay.

707. She hummed a cheerful little ditty as she sewed him into the cocoon.

708. Tears filled his eyes as he looked out over the Coliseum of Rome, remembering how many of his friends had lost their lives there for the sheer entertainment of others.

709. She decided to do something drastic when he mistook her for her twin brother.

710. They didn't realize she could see through the blindfold.

711. She promised to leave when the first crocus bloomed in the spring.

712. I called her my blue angel.

713. He struggled to keep his face from giving away the royal flush in his hand.

714. The spacecraft sent back an image that would rattle the whole world if it were released to the public.

715. Grandma spanked me with her fuzzy slipper.

716. She awakened to the sound of _____.

717. The pain was excruciating, but if I cried out, they would find me.

718. I faced the audience, about to give a speech that was bound to end my career.

719. It was just supposed to be a simple tummy tuck.

720. The tumor was benign, but she withheld that information from him.

721. They found a tunnel that led to the back lot of the amusement park.

722. In all the commotion, no one noticed her slip out of the room.

723. He waited nervously at the tollbooth.

724. The doctor removed the bandages revealing her new face.

725. I think she ripped my tutu on purpose.

726. Halfway down the stairs she noticed that the front door was standing wide open.

727. He had just popped dinner into the microwave when the phone rang.

728. She inflicted great pain with a simple pair of tweezers.

729. Something told me to go slow and proceed with caution.

730. He walked the beach every night at twilight, searching for something.

731. She felt a twinge of guilt, but knew it was a necessary lie.

732. He was talking in his sleep again, but this time he _____.

733. She shuddered when she saw bloodstains on the keys of the old typewriter.

734. The wagon master insisted we pull out of the wagon train at daybreak.

735. He made sure each divot in his waffle was filled with butter and syrup.

736. He pulled out of Waco like a bat out of—well, you know.

737. Her winsome ways pulled me into her nasty little scheme.

738. His arms encircled my waist from behind, and then tightened sharply.

739. I asked the clerk for a five-o'clock wake-up call, but it never came.

740. We walked into the room hand-in-hand. Whatever they had to say, they could say it to the both of us.

741. "I'll be there in five minutes," he said into the walkie-talkie, "Had to wait for my mom to go to bed."

742. It was the winning ticket. Should I tell him or not?

743. She had lied too many times to count, but this time I believed her.

744. He wondered what they would do now that he had exceeded his life expectancy.

745. The lieutenant refused to submit to her authority.

746. She knew he would place a lien on her father's farm unless she agreed to his proposal.

747. This was a life sentence he didn't intend to serve.

WILL WRITE FOR CHOCOLATE   Copyright©2010 Debbie Ridpath Ohi

748. I didn't believe in the boogeyman, but someone was definitely hiding under my bed.

749. She found a receipt in his pocket for _____.

750. She pulled the plug on the life raft and watched it deflate, carrying the body to the bottom of the sea.

751. With just seconds to go before liftoff, he had a sudden premonition that something was going to go terribly wrong.

752. He knew that he was nothing more than her current pet project.

753. He had not seen his daughter since she was three months old.

754. She climbed the circular staircase in the old abandoned lighthouse.

755. He hadn't expected to encounter sabotage in culinary school.

756. "That's your alibi?" he said, "You spent the night in the crapper?"

757. He broke up with her five minutes before the big audition.

758. "Do you think you could loan me your children for about an hour?" he asked.

759. She didn't seem to appreciate the Weight Watcher coupons I had tucked inside her birthday card.

760. He heard the ice crack just before the shanty began to sink.

761. Spending my days inside a chicken suit is not eggzactly how I planned my summer.

762. He climbed the fence and dropped to the ground inside the cemetery.

763. She let the letter lay on the table for hours before she got up enough nerve to open it.

764. Who would have thought his fifteen minutes of fame would come on the day he was born.

765. She always requested exactly three ice cubes in her glass.

766. They agreed on everything but where they would scatter the ashes.

767. The resemblance was remarkable, but they denied being related.

768. She sat on a lily pad trying to remember how to reverse the spell.

769. They couldn't link him to the crime unless they found the missing tube of lipstick.

770. Her humble home had become a secret haven for the rich and famous visiting Las Vegas.

771. "Why are you acting as if we've never met?" she asked.

772. He moved through the halls undetected and slipped into the door marked Housekeeping.

773. She couldn't look him in the eye because _____..

774. They discovered the discrepancies during an annual audit and all of the evidence pointed to me.

775. How could she say kissing another man was an accident?

776. He stuffed all the money into his backpack and hit the road.

777. He propped the gun up on a log, ignoring the pain in his right shoulder, and waited for the right moment.

778. He jimmied the lock and let himself into the darkened house. He could hear the shower running upstairs.

779. They lined up around the block just to get an autograph from the imposter.

780. He made the rounds in his golf cart, pistol strapped to his side, hoping for a little action.

781. She opened the mailbox, reached her hand in and felt a sharp stinging sensation.

782. Watermelon juice dripped down his arms and onto his dirty bare feet.

783. He locked me in a room the size of a closet. All the walls were covered with mirrors.

784. He boarded the train bound for Nashville with thirty dollars in his pocket and a suitcase full of dreams.

785. They pulled the motor home off the paved road and drove back into the forest several miles.

786. The owner of the toy shop gave me an odd looking stone from the display case. He said I could keep it.

787. The captain of the charter boat asked for the passengers' cell phones and threw them into the river.

788. The wedding was held in a dark and dreary castle.

789. She found a book under the cushion of her husband' chair entitled The Benefits of Bigamy.

790. She stood in the rain at the bus stop holding a suitcase and a newborn.

791. She noticed lipstick on the edge of her glass, but she wasn't wearing lipstick.

792. The lock on the shed door was rusted shut, but he could hear movement inside.

793. He was mortified. The last thing he wanted to do on the first day of school was _____.

794. The old shack on the beach would serve him well for the next three months.

795. She rummaged through her mother-in-law's purse looking for her stolen credit card.

796. She removed her scarf to reveal her newly shaven and tattooed head.

797. It was disgusting how she couldn't pass a mirror without admiring the results of her recent surgery.

798. He took her money, her phone, her keys and her passport, then drove her to a remote village, removed the handcuffs and made her get out of the car.

799. The old brick schoolhouse was crumbling, the windows were broken and leafless vines covered the walls.

800. I waited by the carousel for him for three hours, but he never came.

801. The room had been freshly painted, but the stains still showed through.

802. She pulled a tiny dog from her handbag, handed it to the little girl and walked away.

803. Hundreds of pigeons surrounded her, nipping at her toes and ankles.

804. She bought the statue at a white elephant sale, but something was rattling inside.

805. She pushed the button and the pendant popped open to reveal a tiny folded piece of paper.

806. He poked at the haystack with a pitchfork. I prayed he wouldn't hit me.

807. Her home was a haven for misfits like me.

808. The machine went haywire. Dials started spinning backward, smoke rolled from the back and then it exploded.

809. We held hands, laughed and sang on the hayride, having no idea what lay in store for us once we reached the old barn.

810. Her headaches were getting more frequent and more intense.

811. She almost gagged when he said it was headcheese. She didn't even want to know what was in it.

812. His foot slipped and he fell headfirst into the irrigation ditch, losing consciousness.

813. The door had not been unlocked since _____.

814. The music was blasting through her headphones as she enjoyed her morning jog. She never heard what came next.

815. She leaned back on the headrest and closed her eyes, swollen from so much crying.

816. He flipped a quarter into the air. "Heads or tails?" he asked. She called tails and said a quick prayer before it hit the ground.

817. Our governess was a straight-laced, no-nonsense woman until our parents left for an extended vacation in Europe.

818. "Don't be so grabby," Granny said, rapping my knuckles with a wooden spoon. "There's plenty enough for everybody."

819. She held the gown to her and twirled across the floor. She couldn't wait for the dance.

820. Three students in her class had contracted the disease so far.

821. He said he had graduated from a prestigious law school, but they had no record of his attendance.

822. He was strangely drawn to the grand piano in the corner of the concert hall.

823. She lifted the grasshopper to her lips.

824. There was nothing more gratifying than watching him admit to the boss that it had been my idea all along.

825. She wondered who this stranger was, crying at her mother's grave.

826. With enough grease paint and a red rubber nose, he might be able to disguise the fact that his heart was breaking.

827. I had never met my great aunt, but I had heard all the hilarious family stories.

828. She was a groupie and she was found dead in his dressing room.

829. He has visited Ground Zero every single day since the great tragedy.

830. A strange stillness closed in once he entered the small grove of trees in the meadow.

831. No one could ever accuse her of being _____.

832. He had what folks call a lazy eye, but the kids around our town called it his evil eye.

833. He led the way down the narrow ledge at the mouth of the cave. It would be many days before the hikers were seen again.

834. "I need to go feed the kids," she said, opening the dungeon door.

835. The air was brisk and the leaves were crisp under my feet as I carried a fresh pumpkin pie through the woods to the little hidden cabin in the glen.

836. I noticed he was left-handed. My sister's attacker had also been left-handed.

837. He had one shot to get this picture. If he was discovered, neither he nor the picture would ever make it back to the newspaper office.

838. It was just psoriasis, but I was so sick of the constant questions, I started telling people it was leprosy.

839. The library was their safe haven after becoming homeless.

840. He was the first person on the scene. One look told him who had done it, so he slipped the incriminating evidence into his pocket.

841. He had picked up enough of the lingo to know that they were talking about robbing him.

842. He rifled through the glove compartment until he found the registration, noted the owner's home address, then put everything back in place before the driver returned to the car.

843. They were little people, no more than six inches high with chameleon-like skin.

844. He climbed the ladder, greased the top three rungs, then climbed back down and hid in the bushes.

845. He got the call in the middle of rush hour traffic. He had to make it to the hospital before it was too late.

846. The sarcophagus was en route to the museum when the delivery van broke down.

847. He sat on a crate on the sidewalk and played his guitar. Very few people realized who he was.

848. Orchard Lane was a quiet street, except for an occasional murder.

849. The only person who could penetrate her Alzheimer's ridden mind was her rebellious granddaughter.

850. She ripped out every stitch of the sweater she had been knitting.

851. The choir director made her so mad she wanted to cuss right there in church.

852. She covered the box of rat poison in bright gift wrap and tied on a huge bow.

853. He spit on the ground, then looked me straight in the eye and said, "_____."

854. She gave the cab driver the customary tip, along with a generous piece of her mind.

855. The sign above her register said, "The Customer Is Always Right", but this one was testing her last nerve.

856. His cutthroat business practices had earned him a corner office in the penthouse, but it had also just cost him his best friend.

857. He had always wanted to rescue a damsel in distress, but once he did, he vowed never to make that mistake again.

858. He led me through the dank corridors of the prison to the cell that had once held my great-grandfather.

859. This time she dared to speak up for herself and it caught him by surprise.

860. The date stamp on the photograph proved the picture had been taken after she had disappeared.

861. His daughter had no idea that her fiancé was a scoundrel and she probably wouldn't believe him if he told her.

862. Dawn broke over the valley as the townspeople prepared for the biggest fight of their lives.

863. She dropped the children off at daycare, picked up a cappuccino at the coffee shop and headed for the morgue.

864. The road dead-ended at the cliffs above the lake, but he never hit the brakes.

865. She was shocked when she reviewed the pictures on her digital camera.

866. He knew he shouldn't read her diary.

867. She bought a train ticket to the end of the line. Wherever it stopped, that's where she would start her new life.

868. As soon as the elevator door shut, they started to argue violently.

869. He was drop-dead gorgeous and rich as Rockefeller, but she wouldn't give him the time of day.

870.   She came face-to-face with his ex-wife in the obstetrician's office.

871.   They topped the mountain, dismounted and let the horses graze while father and son looked out over the Colorado countryside.

872.   She absentmindedly ran the stop sign and almost hit a car. Now that same car was tailgating her.

873.   She was called away from her table at the restaurant to take a phone call. When she returned, she was halfway through her sandwich before she realized that she had sat down at the wrong table.

874.   The teacher made him sit with the girls for the rest of the afternoon.

875.   His sniffling was driving her crazy.

876.   The garbage bag broke as he threw it into the truck, spilling its contents onto the road.

877.   I knew I had to arrest her for domestic violence, but had to laugh when I saw him duct-taped to the toilet.

878.   The salesman didn't know what to say when the customers asked if he could give them a few minutes alone to try out the backseat.

879.   He saw the words "Guess Who" scrawled across his bathroom mirror in bright pink lipstick.

880.   He picked up a hitchhiker in Phoenix. She kicked him out of his own truck in Flagstaff.

881.   She crossed the room and tripped over a loose board in the floor. The board had not been loose yesterday.

882.   The teacher noticed an ugly bruise on the boy's face.

883.   She loosened two spark plugs, and then drove straight to the garage where he worked.

884.   She had just made her weekly deposit when the gunman entered the bank.

885.   She dialed his number three times, but every time he answered, she hung up.

886. Who does their laundry at the Laundromat at three o'clock in the morning? Me, that's who.

887. It even smelled like a crime scene.

888. Never in all her life would she have imagined that today she would be _____.

889. He struggled to free his baby from the car seat, pushed him out through the front windshield and then climbed out after him.

890. She woke to find that someone had slipped a key under the locked bedroom door.

891. They were enjoying their air-boat ride through the everglades when suddenly the engine sputtered and died.

892. She painted from memory, after having lost her eyesight many years ago.

893. She refused to allow fresh flowers in the house.

894. Her hair-brained escapades had been getting me in trouble for years. This one almost got me killed.

895. He arranged a hot air balloon ride for my birthday.

896. A week ago I could have turned right back around and gone home, now I could never go home again.

897. He had gotten away with murder. If you're rich enough or famous enough, you can do that.

898. She hired a carpenter to build a secret room between the first and second bedrooms on the third floor.

899. He had always thought it would be fun to be a castaway on a deserted island—until now.

900. A pair of majestic stone lions stood guard at the entrance to the castle, but security cameras had recently been installed in their eyes.

901. She was used to walking in the bush alone, but this time she only thought she was alone.

902. He wandered through the noisy crowd in the marketplace watching the pretty American woman. Then he saw her discreetly slip something into the pocket of a passing businessman.

903. He was walking home when a man slipped out of a dark alley, stuck a gun in his back and demanded his wallet. This was the third time he'd been mugged, but this time he had a surprise in store for the thug.

904. She was on a mission trip, bringing aid to the children who lived in the garbage dumps of Mexico City. When it came time to leave, she couldn't make herself leave the children.

905. She was enjoying the lavish buffet and the hula dancers at the luau when a native child slipped up and handed her a note.

906. Sweat trickled down the nape of her neck as she stood on the veranda and looked out over the tobacco fields of the old plantation.

907. He stood, tears streaming down his face, before the Wailing Wall, rolled the paper on which he had written his prayer and pushed it into a crevice of the wall.

908. He stuffed the bag of jewels inside the fish, wrapped it and put it in the freezer.

909. He grew his hair and beard, donned the clothes he had picked up at a thrift store and headed for the streets and alleys of New York City with nothing in his pocket but a pencil and a pad of paper.

910. He opened his lunchbox and found a note from his mom telling him to come straight home after school, but he had other plans..

911. They had been hiking in Yellowstone Park for days before they came upon a grove filled with dead bear carcasses—all of them missing only their paws.

912. She lay in the middle of the floor in a pool of _____.

913. They threw up their arms and screamed like little girls when the

roller coaster topped the highest hill, but their screams turned to sheer terror when the safety bar flipped up just as they began to descend.

914.   She sat unobtrusively to the left of the king's throne and played a soothing melody on her lute.

915.   A magpie flew through the open window and landed on her dressing table. She watched in horror as it snatched her engagement ring and flew off.

916.   She ran her fingers over the bark of the tree tracing the heart and initials they had carved a lifetime ago.

917.   He didn't realize until he was 6 years old that not everyone could hear another person's thoughts.

918.   She peeked through the gaps in the wooden walls of the boathouse.

919.   The notice on the school bulletin board said, "Silly Sara loves Stinky McFee." She knew who had tacked it there and she intended to make them pay.

920.   Her parents told her nothing before dropping her off at the home of an aunt she had never met. They said they would be back in a month.

921.   "I'm glad you can joke about this," she said as she trimmed her fast-growing beard.

922.   She admired the beautiful chandelier in the foyer and the grand staircase leading to the balcony above. She didn't belong in a place like this.

923.   She could have told him how the window broke, but she refused to betray her best friend.

924.   I turned 13 in the hospital, but it was the best birthday party I ever had.

925.   She could hear the murmur of voices at the foot of the stairs as her eyes frantically swept the room for a hiding place.

926. The screen went black, someone screamed and then pandemonium broke out in the theater.

927. I backed out of the driveway carefully, but a car careened around the curve and hit me. The driver jumped from the car and ran, but not before I recognized him as our senior class president.

928. We devoured the whole plate of cookies before realizing that Mom had made them for the women's club bake sale.

929. They poured over the maps of the Canadian wilderness, planning a route that would keep them far from civilization and possible arrest. By the time it was all said and done, they would have welcomed the safety of a prison cell.

930. As soon as his mother shut the bedroom door, he slipped out of bed and signaled out the window with a flashlight.

931. Once again, he had his nose buried in a book.

932. I had failed, but I would try again and again and again.

933. She had one minute to make up her mind.

934. Tangled thoughts wove themselves around her heart.

935. She skipped over and handed me a bouquet of weeds and grass.

936. She tried spending quiet time with God, but the silence from heaven was deafening.

937. I thought of myself as an aimless wanderer, never realizing that my steps were being ordered by someone else.

938. My friend calls them 911 prayers. I hope they work, because this was a real emergency!

939. I found her journal on the park bench. After reading it, I knew I had to find her.

940. I found myself praying in a church, but I had no recollection of how I had gotten there.

941. I wandered through the graveyard reading the headstones until one stopped me dead in my tracks.

942. A deep peace settled over me as soon as I realized the plane was going down.

943. He was a diamond in the rough, but with a little work we could pull it off.

944. I wanted to sympathize with her, but inwardly I was elated that they had broken up.

945. God may have forgiven him, but I didn't know if I ever could.

946. He had no idea that the contraption he was tinkering with would change his life in the next five minutes.

947. I swear my mother could read minds!

948. I felt like someone had just reissued me a spine.

949. Her weapon of choice? Words!

950. She looked at the caller ID...he had found her!

951. Everything I had said was true, but I never thought it would get back to her.

952. I refused to take a backseat to his hunting buddies.

953. I decided to forego the services of a tour guide and show myself around the ancient city.

954. The serenity of her ocean blue eyes disguised the dangerous undercurrent lurking behind them.

955. The travel agent had described it as a quaint, country cottage.

956. Something in my gut told me that I needed to get home immediately.

957. He was too busy to work me into his schedule.

958. I had made the appointment, but would I be brave enough to keep it?

959. With a surge of adrenaline, I lifted the log off her leg.

960. Wanting to be a writer so bad I could taste it, I decided to get the publisher's attention one way or another.

961. Anxious thoughts whirled around me like a dirt devil in the Arizona desert.

962. With that one sentence, an unexpected life had been thrust upon me.

963. I saw my mother's face flash across the television screen just as I hit the power button on the remote to find something to watch besides the ten-o'clock news.

964. "This is a hold-up," he said. And I burst out laughing.

965. She was just as sweet and refreshing as the iced-tea she had served me.

966. The first time I put it to my lips, I was hooked!

967. He had been a tyrant all his life, so why was he being so nice now?

968. He was 89 years old and usually very quiet, but today he felt like talking.

969. She invited me into her life, and since that day mine has never been the same.

970. I believed that love was not something you fell into and out of, but a learned behavior, an acquired skill until I laid eyes on the tenant in apartment 3A.

971. My plan was to remain unknown.

972. The ruffles on her prom dress fluttered in the breeze as she sat crying on the top row of the football bleachers.

973. I had won a week's vacation at the beach!

974. He had purchased her at the slave market, but he would never own her.

975. She left behind a legacy of faith—a faith that would accomplish more than she would ever know.

976. He knew a lot about women, but he still didn't understand them.

977. "He's your father," she said as she walked away.

978. Wild blows the wind in the heart of a cowboy.

979. She followed the direction of his stare and once again it was fixed on another woman.

980. I remembered the voice of God speaking to me while I was yet in my mother's womb.

981. I had devised the perfect payback for the way he had made fun of me in front of the class.

982. "You have two choices," he said. "Do it my way or suffer the consequences."

983. I had walked the aisle, kissed the groom, danced the dance and eaten the cake, but _____.

984. She had begun to imagine what life with him would be like.

985. Her hands were freezing and she was losing her grip.

986. I tried to embrace reality, but fantasy kept creeping into my head.

987. She had long ago stopped worrying about what others thought.

988. A scorching wind blew across the desert floor to where she lay in the sand.

989. He had screwed up his courage and poured his heart out. The next move was hers.

990. "Old habits die hard," he said, wrapping his arms around her.

991. He flinched at the sound of her voice.

992. "Look it up in the dictionary!" she said, slamming down the receiver.

993. It was a horrible scene and yet my eyes were drawn to it like a magnet.

994. "Grab it quick, and let's get out of here," he said when she was out of earshot.

995. I was tired and cranky and in no mood for romance.

996. She had created a safe place for herself, a haven from the storms of life, but dark clouds were gathering on the horizon.

997. "I guess you can have your cake and eat it, too," she said.

998. "Some kids are just mistakes," she said with a shrug of her shoulders.

999. The steady pecking of the keyboard meant things were going well with his writing, but why wouldn't he let her read the story?

1000. She placed the item on the checkout conveyor, avoiding the eyes of the clerk.

1001. Friend or foe? She couldn't decide which one described him best.

About The Author

Jan Christiansen is a freelance writer, web designer, blogger, and author of Wake Up Your Muse - 1001 Story Starters for Fiction Writers, published by Written World Communications, and two devotional books, More of Him, Less of Me and Desert Morsels. Her work appears in Love is a Verb Devotional by Gary Chapman and in several online publications.

Jan is the founder of Inspired Ink Writers Group and is a member of ACFW. She is currently working on her first novel, an inspirational story set in the small fictional town of Carter's Creek, Ohio. You can visit her at http://www.wakeupyourmuse.com/ and at her personal website.

About The Illustrator

Debbie Ridpath Ohi is a freelance writer & illustrator whose blogs and webcomics for writers include Inkygirl.com and WillWriteForChocolate. com. She is author of THE WRITER'S ONLINE MARKETPLACE (Writer's Digest Books) and illustrator of I'M BORED (Author: Michael Ian Black, Simon & Schuster 2012). Represented by Ginger Knowlton of Curtis Brown. Twitter: @ inkyelbows. URL: DebbieOhi.com.

Photo by Jeff Ridpath

CPSIA information can be obtained at www.ICGtesting.com
Printed in the USA
BVOW051300121011

273393BV00006B/3/P